Guide to Kubernetes

Practical Guide

A. De Quattro

Copyright © 2024

Practical Guide

1.Introduction

Kubernetes is an open-source platform designed to automate the deployment, management, and scaling of containerized applications. Originally developed by Google and donated to the Cloud Native Computing Foundation (CNCF), Kubernetes is now one of the most widely used tools for orchestrating and managing container-based infrastructure, with Docker being the most common containerization technology.

The popularity of Kubernetes is due to its ability to abstract and manage complex infrastructures, making it easier for developers and system administrators to manage container clusters at scale. Instead of manually handling the provisioning and lifecycle of containers, Kubernetes offers a decentralized and scalable architecture that automates deployment, load balancing, networking, storage, and other operational aspects.

In simple terms, Kubernetes addresses critical issues such as:

- **Container Orchestration**: Schedules and coordinates containers within distributed clusters, ensuring they run on the right nodes and responding to events like failures and load spikes.

- **Automated Scalability**: Automatically scales resources to respond to demand fluctuations, optimizing infrastructure usage.

- **Resilience**: Ensures high availability of applications, reducing downtime by automatically restarting failed containers and load balancing.

- **Seamless Updates**: Allows updating running applications without downtime through processes like rolling updates.

History and Evolution

Kubernetes originated from an internal Google project known as **Borg**, a system that managed thousands of containers at scale for the company's internal services. Google, recognizing the need to share this technology with the open-source community, launched Kubernetes in 2014, bringing the best practices derived from Borg into an open-source ecosystem.

Since its initial release, Kubernetes has undergone significant evolution. Its early versions had limited features and were less stable, but the ecosystem rapidly expanded with contributions from around the world. In 2015, Kubernetes was donated to the **Cloud Native Computing Foundation (CNCF)**, an organization that promotes the development of cloud-native technologies. This move strengthened its role in the open-source world and accelerated its development.

Subsequent versions of Kubernetes introduced advanced features such as **dynamic networking**, **persistent storage support**, **advanced logging services**, and security tools like **pod security policies**. The project's evolution has made Kubernetes the leading platform for container orchestration, adopted by many companies worldwide, from startups to large enterprises.

Today, Kubernetes supports a wide variety of distributed applications and microservices, allowing integration with many cloud technologies like Amazon Web Services (AWS), Google Cloud Platform (GCP), Microsoft Azure, and other private and public platforms. Additionally, it has fostered the development of entire ecosystems of related open-source projects, such as Helm, Prometheus, and others.

Kubernetes Architecture

Kubernetes is designed with a modular and distributed architecture. Its architecture is based on a set of nodes that form a **cluster**. Each Kubernetes cluster consists mainly of two types of nodes:

1. **Master Nodes**: Responsible for managing and controlling the cluster. The master node coordinates the overall behavior of the system and hosts various components like the API server, controller manager, and etcd.

2. **Worker Nodes**: Run the application containers managed by Kubernetes. Each worker node hosts one or more **Pods**, the smallest executable unit in Kubernetes.

The Kubernetes architecture consists of the following main components:

- **API Server**: It is the front-end of Kubernetes. It handles client requests (usually through `kubectl`) and communicates with various internal components. Every change to the infrastructure passes through the API Server.

- **Etcd**: It is a distributed key-value store used to store the cluster configuration data. It is essential for ensuring consistency and availability of critical information on a global scale.

- **Controller Manager**: Manages controllers that monitor the state of the cluster and initiate actions to ensure that the infrastructure reaches the desired state (e.g., resizing pods or recovering failed nodes).

- **Scheduler**: The component that decides which nodes new pods will run on. It uses a set of predefined rules to optimize resource allocation based on user-defined constraints.

- **Kubelet**: An agent that runs on each worker node. The Kubelet receives instructions from the master node and ensures that containers are running correctly on the nodes.

- **Kube Proxy**: Manages networking rules within each node and ensures that pods can communicate with each other and with the outside.

- **Pod**: The smallest unit in Kubernetes. A pod represents one or more containers that run together with shared resources (e.g., network and storage). Each pod is highly ephemeral: it can be created, destroyed, and moved across different nodes with no noticeable interruptions to the user.

Fundamental Components

In the overall Kubernetes system, there are some key concepts and components that are essential to understand:

- **Namespace**: Provides a logical isolation space to organize and manage resources within a cluster. It is used to separate projects or workgroups.

- **ReplicaSet**: Ensures that a specific

number of replicas of a pod are running at all times.

- **Deployment**: A high-level resource that manages the creation and scaling of ReplicaSets. It allows for progressive updates (rolling updates) without disrupting the service.

- **Service**: Defines an access rule for pods, exposing them both internally within the cluster and externally.

- **ConfigMap** and **Secret**: Used to manage configurations and credentials external to the pods securely.

- **Ingress**: An object that manages HTTP/S access to services within the cluster, facilitating request routing.

Kubernetes Installation

The installation of Kubernetes varies depending on the environment and chosen tools. Depending on needs, one can opt for local installations on a single machine (useful for development) or deployment on distributed cloud infrastructure. Below, we will examine the prerequisites and main options for installing Kubernetes.

Prerequisites

Before installing Kubernetes, a series of technical prerequisites must be met. These include:

1. **Operating Systems**: Kubernetes can run on various Linux distributions, including Ubuntu, CentOS, and Fedora. Additionally, there are versions for Windows, but Linux is preferred for production nodes.

2. **Virtualization or Containerization Tools**:

   - Docker or a runtime compatible with the Container Runtime Interface (CRI).

3. **Networking**: Kubernetes nodes must be able to communicate with each other without firewall restrictions and with internal connectivity. Additionally, DNS must be set up or **CoreDNS** must be used.

4. **Hardware**: For a production cluster, it is recommended to have at least 3 master nodes for redundancy and fault tolerance, along with sufficient CPU, RAM, and storage resources.

5. **Privileged Access**: During installation, root or sudo permissions will be needed to configure system components.

6. **Command-line Utilities**:

- `kubectl`: The official tool for interacting with the cluster.

  - `kubeadm`: Used to initialize and configure Kubernetes clusters on physical or virtual servers.

Installation Options

Minikube

Minikube is a tool that allows you to create a local Kubernetes cluster on a single virtual machine, making it ideal for development or testing environments. It is the easiest way to get started with Kubernetes without setting up a full cluster.

The advantages of Minikube include:

- Ease of use: Requires few commands for installation and configuration.
- Compatibility: Supports multiple

hypervisors like VirtualBox, VMware, and KVM.

- Ability to emulate a full Kubernetes environment locally.

The steps for installing Minikube include:

1. Install `kubectl`, the command-line interface.

2. Download Minikube and start a virtual machine with Kubernetes.

3. Verify the cluster with commands like `kubectl cluster-info`.

Kubeadm

Kubeadm is an official tool for installing and configuring Kubernetes on distributed clusters. It is designed to simplify the process of bootstrapping a cluster across multiple nodes, providing a guided flow for initializing the cluster.

The main steps include:

1. **Initialize the cluster**: `kubeadm init` initializes the master node and generates the tokens needed to add other nodes.

2. **Add worker nodes**: Use `kubeadm join` to add worker nodes to the cluster.

3. **Configure networking and pod overlay**: After initialization, you need to configure networking, typically using tools like Flannel or Calico.

Kubeadm does not manage production services like load balancing or cluster lifecycle management, which must be configured separately.

Kops

Kops (Kubernetes Operations) is an

open-source tool that simplifies the installation, management, and upgrading of Kubernetes clusters on cloud environments, particularly on **Amazon Web Services (AWS)**.

Kops allows you to:

- Create and configure highly available clusters on AWS.

- Perform rolling updates of cluster nodes.

- Automate management of AWS resources related to the cluster, such as subnets and load balancers.

The initial setup of Kops includes:

1. **Create a DNS domain**: Kops uses DNS to discover cluster nodes.

2. **Install kops and kubectl**.

3. **Create the cluster**: Use the `kops create cluster` command to configure the entire

AWS cluster.

Amazon EKS

Amazon Elastic Kubernetes Service (EKS) is a managed service that simplifies running Kubernetes on AWS. With EKS, Amazon handles the management of master nodes and other underlying infrastructure, leaving users to manage worker nodes.

The advantages of EKS include:

- Native integration with other AWS services like IAM and VPC.

- Managed updates of cluster components.

- Redundancy and high availability for master nodes.

Google GKE

Google Kubernetes Engine (GKE) is a managed service offered by Google Cloud Platform. As Kubernetes originated at Google, GKE is often considered one of the best environments for running Kubernetes, thanks to its tight integration with Google infrastructure.

The strengths of GKE include:

- Support for cluster autoscaling.

- Integration with Stackdriver for monitoring.

- Advanced support for networking and security policies.

Azure AKS

**Azure Kubernetes

Service (AKS)** is Microsoft's Azure offering for Kubernetes. AKS is a managed service that handles provisioning, monitoring, and updating the cluster.

The benefits of AKS include:

- Integration with Active Directory for identity management.

- Automation of cluster patching and updates.

- Integration with tools like Azure Monitor for tracking and telemetry.

Initial Configuration

After installation, it is necessary to configure the cluster to meet the specific needs of the environment. The steps include:

1. **Set up networking**: Install a network plugin like Flannel or Calico to enable communication between pods.

2. **Set up Access Control (RBAC)**: Configure roles and permissions needed for secure access to cluster components.

3. **Manage storage**: Create storage classes and manage persistent volumes for applications that require them.

4. **Monitoring and logging**: Configure tools like Prometheus and Grafana to monitor cluster status and collect metrics.

With these steps, the Kubernetes cluster will be ready to run containerized applications in a scalable and highly available environment.

2. Kubernetes: Fundamental Concepts

In Kubernetes, fundamental concepts are essential for managing and orchestrating containerized applications. These concepts provide the necessary tools to manage resources, configurations, and the state of applications within a cluster. In this guide, we will delve into the concepts of **Pod**, **ReplicaSet**, **Deployment**, **Namespace**, **Service**, **ConfigMap and Secret**, **Volumes and Persistence**, **StatefulSet**, and **DaemonSet**, with both theoretical and practical details.

Pod

What is a Pod?

A **Pod** is the basic execution unit in Kubernetes. It represents an instance of one or more containerized applications that share the same **network namespace** and

storage, such as persistent volumes. A Pod can contain one or more containers, but in most cases, it contains a single container. When a Pod includes multiple containers, these containers share resources like networking and storage, but each container runs as a separate process.

Pods are designed to be **ephemeral**, meaning they are not meant to be durable. If a Pod is terminated, Kubernetes can create a new Pod to replace it, but the new Pod will not be an exact replica of the previous one (it will have a unique ID and may be located on a different node). This is one of the reasons Kubernetes encourages using **Deployments** or **ReplicaSets** to manage groups of Pods.

Pod Example

An example of a Pod running a single Nginx container would be:

```yaml
apiVersion: v1
kind: Pod
metadata:
  name: nginx-pod
spec:
  containers:
  - name: nginx-container
    image: nginx:latest
    ports:
    - containerPort: 80
```

In this example:

- **apiVersion**: The API version being used.

- **kind**: The type of resource, in this case, `Pod`.

- **metadata**: Defines the name of the Pod.

- **spec**: Specifies the Pod configuration, including the containers.

- **containers**: Contains the list of containers within the Pod. In this case, there is one container called `nginx-container` using the `nginx:latest` image.

Pod Features

- **Resource sharing**: All containers within a Pod share the same IP address, ports, and volumes.

- **Ephemeral**: Pods are not persistent; they are destroyed and recreated as needed.

- **Isolation**: Each Pod is isolated from other Pods and has its own runtime environment.

ReplicaSet

What is a ReplicaSet?

A **ReplicaSet** is a Kubernetes resource that ensures a specific number of Pod replicas are running at any given time. ReplicaSet is the successor to **ReplicationController** but offers additional features such as support for label selector-based sets.

A ReplicaSet monitors the Pods, and if any fail, it creates new Pods to replace them. The goal is to maintain the exact number of running replicas at all times. If a Pod fails, a new Pod is automatically created to maintain the desired replica count.

ReplicaSet Example

Below is an example of a ReplicaSet that ensures there are always 3 replicas of an Nginx Pod running:

```yaml
apiVersion: apps/v1
kind: ReplicaSet
metadata:
  name: nginx-replicaset
spec:
  replicas: 3
  selector:
    matchLabels:
      app: nginx
  template:
    metadata:
      labels:
        app: nginx
    spec:
      containers:
      - name: nginx
        image: nginx:latest
```

      ports:

      - containerPort: 80
```

In this example:

- **replicas**: Specifies the desired number of replicas (3 in this case).

- **selector**: Defines a label selector that indicates which Pods the ReplicaSet should monitor. The selector looks for all Pods with the label `app: nginx`.

- **template**: A template for the new Pods to be created. In this case, each Pod will have an Nginx container.

### ReplicaSet Features

- **Redundancy and High Availability**: ReplicaSet maintains a stable number of Pods, ensuring service continuity.
```

- **Self-healing**: If a Pod fails, a new one is automatically created.

- **Scalability**: The number of replicas can be changed at any time by updating the `replicas` field.

Deployment

What is a Deployment?

A **Deployment** is a Kubernetes resource that manages the lifecycle of applications. A Deployment is a higher-level resource than a ReplicaSet, and it allows for easy management of complex operations like updates, rollbacks, scaling, and more on Pods.

Deployments are commonly used to orchestrate **rolling updates** of Pods, which means gradually updating Pods to minimize downtime. Kubernetes updates Pods one at a time or in small batches, removing Pods with the old version and replacing them with those using the new version.

Deployment Example

Here's an example of a Deployment that creates a ReplicaSet with 3 replicas of an Nginx container:

```yaml
apiVersion: apps/v1
kind: Deployment
metadata:
  name: nginx-deployment
spec:
  replicas: 3
  selector:
    matchLabels:
      app: nginx
  template:
```

```
    metadata:
      labels:
        app: nginx
    spec:
      containers:
      - name: nginx
        image: nginx:1.19.0
        ports:
        - containerPort: 80
```

Deployment Features

- **Rolling updates**: Deployment supports updating Pods without downtime by updating them one at a time.

- **Rollback**: If an update fails, you can roll back to a previous version of the Deployment.

- **Self-healing**: If a Pod fails, Kubernetes automatically creates a new one to replace it.

- **Scalability**: You can resize the number of replicas via a simple command or by updating the Deployment.

An example of a **rolling update** can be performed simply by changing the Docker image in the Deployment. Kubernetes will automatically begin replacing existing Pods with those using the new image:

```yaml
spec:
  containers:
  - name: nginx
    image: nginx:1.20.0
```

Namespace

What is a Namespace?

A **Namespace** provides a logical division within Kubernetes, allowing you to split a single Kubernetes cluster into multiple virtual sub-clusters, each with its own isolated space for resources. Namespaces are useful when managing multiple teams or projects on a single cluster, as they help prevent naming conflicts and provide isolation between different applications.

Namespaces are optional; if no Namespace is specified, Kubernetes uses the default Namespace (`default`). Kubernetes also includes a few predefined Namespaces:

- **kube-system**: For Kubernetes system components.

- **kube-public**: Publicly accessible throughout the cluster.

- **default**: The default Namespace for

resources that don't specify one.

Namespace Example

To create a custom Namespace:

```yaml
apiVersion: v1
kind: Namespace
metadata:
  name: my-namespace
```

You can specify a Namespace when creating a resource, like a Pod or Service, by adding the `namespace` field to the YAML file. For example:

```yaml
```

```
apiVersion: v1
kind: Pod
metadata:
  name: nginx-pod
  namespace: my-namespace
spec:
  containers:
  - name: nginx-container
    image: nginx:latest
```

Namespace Features

- **Isolation**: Provide a level of logical isolation within a cluster.

- **Permission management**: With Namespaces, you can manage access permissions and roles at the Namespace level using tools like RBAC (Role-Based Access Control).

- **Resource management**: Namespaces can be used to apply resource limits (CPU, memory) for teams or projects sharing the same cluster.

3. Networking in Kubernetes

Networking in Kubernetes is a crucial topic for running distributed applications. Unlike traditional environments where networking is handled at the virtual machine or physical server level, in Kubernetes, the network must connect containers, Pods, nodes, and applications across a dynamic, distributed network. This ensures that containers can communicate with each other and with external services seamlessly, even in a scalable and orchestrated environment.

In this guide, we will cover the following topics:

- Kubernetes Network Model

- Services and Endpoints

- Ingress Controller and Ingress

- DNS in Kubernetes

- Network Policies

Kubernetes Network Model

Key Concepts of the Network Model

The **Kubernetes network model** is designed to be simple and flexible, but it hides many complexities to ensure the network remains transparent to developers and system operators. This model is based on a few key concepts:

1. **Each Pod has its own IP**: Every Pod in Kubernetes receives a unique IP address within the cluster. This IP address is used to communicate with other Pods, containers, and services within the same cluster.

2. **Pod-to-Pod Communication**: All Pods in a Kubernetes cluster can communicate directly with each other without using Network Address Translation (NAT). This means any Pod can reach another Pod simply by using its IP address.

3. **Pod-to-Service Communication**: Pods can communicate with Services, which serve as a stable access point for a group of Pods. A Service creates an endpoint with a virtual IP, known as **ClusterIP**, which remains constant even as the Pods associated with the Service change.

4. **Node-to-Node Communication**: Kubernetes allows direct communication between nodes. Pods on different nodes can communicate with each other as if they were on the same network, meaning NAT is not required.

Kubernetes Network Model: Philosophy

The Kubernetes network model follows a set of core requirements that must be met by any networking solution compatible with Kubernetes:

- All containers can communicate with each other without needing to configure NAT.

- All nodes can communicate with all Pods without requiring NAT.

- Pods see their own IP addresses as they are seen by other Pods.

Kubernetes Network Solutions

Kubernetes does not directly implement a network, but it leaves users the freedom to choose a networking solution that meets the network model's requirements. Some common network solutions are:

- **Flannel**: A simple network solution that uses VXLAN-based overlay networks to connect Pods across different nodes.

- **Calico**: Provides both networking and network security using a BGP (Border Gateway Protocol) approach to connect Pods without an overlay network.

- **Weave**: Another overlay network solution that provides secure networking between containers.

- **Cilium**: An advanced solution that uses eBPF (Extended Berkeley Packet Filter) to manage network policies and security.

Container-Level Networking

At the container level, Kubernetes uses the **Container Network Interface (CNI)**, a standard defining how network plugins can interact with the Kubernetes runtime. The network solutions mentioned above (Flannel, Calico, Weave) implement CNI to integrate with Kubernetes.

Common Networking Challenges

Setting up networking in Kubernetes can present several challenges, including:

- **IP Address Management**: Since each Pod has its own IP, it is important to manage the available IP address pool properly.

- **Scalability**: As the number of nodes and Pods grows, the network solutions must scale efficiently.

- **Latency and Performance**: In some scenarios, using overlay networks can introduce additional latency. Non-overlay solutions, like Calico, tend to be more efficient.

Services and Endpoints

Services in Kubernetes

A **Service** in Kubernetes is a network abstraction that exposes a group of Pods through a single stable and constant IP address, known as a **ClusterIP**. Services solve the issue of Pods' ephemeral IP addresses since Pods can be destroyed and recreated at any time, changing their IPs.

Types of Services

1. **ClusterIP** (default): Exposes the service only within the cluster. This means only other Pods within the cluster can access the Service via the assigned virtual IP.

2. **NodePort**: Exposes the service on a specific port on each node in the cluster. This allows external access to the service through the node's IP address and the specific port.

3. **LoadBalancer**: Available only in cloud environments, it creates an external load balancer that directs traffic to the Pods associated with the Service.

4. **ExternalName**: Does not map directly to Pods but redirects traffic to an external DNS name.

Example of a ClusterIP Service

```yaml
apiVersion: v1
kind: Service
metadata:
```

```
  name: my-service
spec:
 selector:
  app: my-app
 ports:
  - protocol: TCP
    port: 80
    targetPort: 8080
```

In this example:

- **selector**: Indicates which Pods will be exposed by the Service by selecting those with the label `app: my-app`.

- **ports**: Specifies that the Service will listen on port 80 (the Service port) and forward traffic to port 8080 of the selected Pods.

Endpoints

Endpoints in Kubernetes represent the actual instances (Pods) running an application associated with a Service. When a Service selects a group of Pods, Kubernetes automatically creates an Endpoints object that maps the Pods' IPs to the Service. This allows the Service to know where to send traffic.

Whenever the selected Pods change (for example, if they are recreated or destroyed), the Endpoints are updated accordingly.

Service Affinity

Kubernetes supports configuring affinity between a client and a Pod for a specific period, so that requests from the same client are consistently routed to the same Pod. This concept is referred to as **session affinity** or **sticky sessions**. The default affinity configuration is based on the client's IP address, where Kubernetes routes the traffic from a specific client IP to the same Pod across multiple requests. However, it is also possible to configure affinity based on other criteria if needed.

Example of Service Affinity

Below is an example configuration of a Kubernetes Service with session affinity enabled based on the client's IP (`ClientIP`):

```yaml
apiVersion: v1
kind: Service
metadata:
  name: my-service
spec:
  selector:
    app: my-app
```

```
  ports:
    - protocol: TCP
      port: 80
      targetPort: 8080
  sessionAffinity: ClientIP
```

How Session Affinity Works

- **sessionAffinity**: In the above example, `sessionAffinity: ClientIP` ensures that all requests coming from the same client IP are forwarded to the same Pod. This is useful when you need consistency in handling requests, such as when dealing with user sessions.

- **affinity timeout**: By default, the session affinity in Kubernetes has a timeout period after which the affinity is reset, and the next request might be routed to a different Pod.

This can be beneficial in scenarios such as shopping carts, where multiple requests from the same client (e.g., a user adding items) should always be handled by the same Pod to maintain consistency in the state.

Configuring Session Affinity Timeout

By default, Kubernetes sets the session affinity timeout to 10800 seconds (3 hours). This timeout can be configured as needed:

```yaml
apiVersion: v1
kind: Service
metadata:
  name: my-service
spec:
  selector:
    app: my-app
```

```
  ports:
    - protocol: TCP
      port: 80
      targetPort: 8080
  sessionAffinity: ClientIP
  sessionAffinityConfig:
    clientIP:
      timeoutSeconds: 600  # Set timeout to 10 minutes
```

In this example:

- **sessionAffinityConfig**: Allows further configuration of the session affinity settings.

- **timeoutSeconds**: Sets the duration (in seconds) for which the session affinity should be maintained. In this case, the session affinity will last for 600 seconds (10 minutes) before it resets.

Limitations of Session Affinity

While session affinity can be useful, it is important to be aware of its limitations:

- **Scaling issues**: If a Pod becomes overloaded with traffic from clients tied to its IP, scaling becomes a challenge, as new Pods might not receive traffic while old Pods are overburdened.

- **State management**: Relying too heavily on session affinity can create complications in applications that scale out to multiple Pods, as sessions are tied to individual Pods rather than being shared across all Pods.

- **Pod lifecycle**: If the Pod that a client is tied to is terminated or restarted, the session affinity is broken, and traffic will be rerouted to a different Pod.

By using session affinity, Kubernetes can ensure that client requests remain consistent across sessions, which is particularly useful in stateful applications that need to preserve the user experience across multiple interactions. However, careful consideration should be given to load balancing, scaling, and Pod availability when implementing this feature.

4. Resource Management in Kubernetes

Resource management in Kubernetes is a fundamental aspect to ensure that containerized applications run efficiently and that the cluster's resources are used optimally. Kubernetes offers various tools and mechanisms to define, monitor, and optimize resource usage across Pods and cluster nodes. In this section, we will cover:

- Resource Limits and Requests
- Resource Triage and Optimization
- Scheduling and Affinity/Anti-Affinity
- Node and Pod Autoscaling

Resource Limits and Requests

Resource Requests

Requests in Kubernetes specify the minimum amount of resources (CPU, memory, etc.) that a container needs to function correctly. When a Pod is scheduled onto a node, Kubernetes ensures that the node has at least the requested resources available for that Pod.

For example, if a Pod requests 200m of CPU (where "m" stands for milli-CPU, meaning 200m is 20% of a CPU) and 512Mi of memory, Kubernetes will try to schedule the Pod on a node that has at least these resources free.

Resource Limits

Limits define the maximum amount of resources that a container can consume. If a container attempts to consume more resources than the specified limit, Kubernetes enforces restrictions, potentially terminating the container or limiting its resource usage.

Here's a practical example of resource requests and limits in a YAML configuration file:

```yaml
apiVersion: v1
kind: Pod
metadata:
  name: example-pod
spec:
  containers:
  - name: example-container
    image: nginx
    resources:
      requests:
        memory: "512Mi"
        cpu: "200m"
      limits:
        memory: "1Gi"
```

      cpu: "500m"
```

In this example, the container "example-container" requests at least 512Mi of memory and 200m of CPU but cannot exceed 1Gi of memory and 500m of CPU.

#### What Happens If a Container Exceeds the Limits?

- **CPU Limits**: If a container tries to exceed the CPU limits, Kubernetes throttles the CPU cycles allocated to the container, reducing its performance.

- **Memory Limits**: If a container exceeds its memory limit, Kubernetes may kill the container. This happens because a container consuming too much memory can jeopardize the stability of the entire node.

### Example of Behavior with Limits and
```

Requests

If a node has 2 CPUs and 4Gi of RAM, and there are three Pods: one with requests of 500m and 1Gi, one with requests of 1 CPU and 2Gi, and one with requests of 1 CPU and 2Gi, Kubernetes will attempt to schedule the first two Pods since they fit within the node's resources. However, the third Pod cannot be scheduled on the same node due to insufficient resources.

Namespace-Level Limits

Resource limits can also be set at the namespace level using `LimitRanges`. This allows administrators to manage resource allocation better among different application groups sharing the same cluster.

```yaml
apiVersion: v1
```

```
kind: LimitRange
metadata:
  name: mem-limit-range
spec:
  limits:
  - default:
      memory: 512Mi
    defaultRequest:
      memory: 256Mi
    type: Container
```

In this example, each container in the namespace that does not specify limits or requests will have a default request of 256Mi of memory and a limit of 512Mi.

Resource Triage and Optimization

Resource triage involves monitoring and managing resource usage in the Kubernetes cluster to ensure that applications are using resources optimally and not exceeding the available capacity.

Resource Monitoring

Kubernetes provides native and third-party tools to monitor resource usage at the cluster, node, and Pod levels. Some common tools include:

- **Metrics Server**: Provides real-time CPU and memory usage metrics at the node and Pod levels.

- **Prometheus**: A highly configurable open-source monitoring solution to collect detailed metrics from Kubernetes and containerized applications.

- **Grafana**: Typically used with Prometheus, Grafana provides graphical dashboards to display collected metrics, making resource analysis easier.

Resource Allocation Optimization

Resource optimization refers to adjusting requests and limits to ensure that resources are allocated correctly without waste. Some useful tips include:

- **Analyze application behavior**: Use historical metrics to determine how much CPU and memory are actually being used and adjust the requests accordingly.

- **Avoid over-provisioning requests**: Excessive over-provisioning leads to wasted capacity.

- **Utilize Autoscaling**: Use autoscaling mechanisms to ensure resources grow and shrink with demand.

Scheduling and Affinity/Anti-Affinity

The Kubernetes scheduler is responsible for deciding which node a Pod will be scheduled on. The scheduler aims to optimize the distribution of Pods based on available resources, Pod requests, and specific rules defined by users.

Affinity and Anti-Affinity

Kubernetes allows you to define **affinity** and **anti-affinity** rules to determine where Pods should or should not be scheduled.

- **Affinity**: Defines preferences for where a Pod should be scheduled. For example, you may want Pods to run on nodes with specific labels or be close to other Pods.

- **Anti-Affinity**: Defines where Pods should not be scheduled. This can be used to avoid having multiple instances of an application on the same node, improving resilience.

Example of Affinity

```yaml
apiVersion: apps/v1
kind: Deployment
metadata:
  name: example-deployment
spec:
  replicas: 3
  template:
    spec:
      affinity:
        nodeAffinity:
          requiredDuringSchedulingIgnoredDuringExecution:
            nodeSelectorTerms:
            - matchExpressions:
```

```
      - key: disktype
        operator: In
        values:
        - ssd
  containers:
  - name: example-container
    image: nginx
```

In this example, Kubernetes will prefer nodes with the label `disktype=ssd` to schedule the Pods.

Example of Anti-Affinity

```yaml
apiVersion: apps/v1
kind: Deployment
metadata:
```

```yaml
  name: example-deployment
spec:
  replicas: 3
  template:
    spec:
      affinity:
        podAntiAffinity:
          requiredDuringSchedulingIgnoredDuringExecution:
            labelSelector:
              matchExpressions:
              - key: app
                operator: In
                values:
                - example-app
            topologyKey: "kubernetes.io/hostname"
      containers:
```

```yaml
    - name: example-container
      image: nginx
```

In this example, Kubernetes will attempt to avoid scheduling multiple Pods of the same application on the same node (`topologyKey` defines distribution by hostname).

Resource-Based Scheduling

The Kubernetes scheduler considers resource requests and limits when deciding where to schedule a Pod. If a node doesn't have sufficient resources to meet a Pod's requests, that node will not be selected.

Node and Pod Autoscaling

Kubernetes supports two main types of autoscaling:

- **Horizontal Pod Autoscaler (HPA)**: Automatically scales the number of Pods in a Deployment, ReplicaSet, or StatefulSet based on resource usage, such as CPU or memory.

- **Cluster Autoscaler**: Adds or removes nodes from the cluster based on resource demand.

Horizontal Pod Autoscaler (HPA)

The HPA automatically scales the number of Pods based on metrics such as CPU usage or custom metrics. Here's an example HPA configuration based on CPU usage:

```yaml
apiVersion: autoscaling/v1
kind: HorizontalPodAutoscaler
metadata:
  name: example-hpa
```

```yaml
spec:
  scaleTargetRef:
    apiVersion: apps/v1
    kind: Deployment
    name: example-deployment
  minReplicas: 2
  maxReplicas: 10
  targetCPUUtilizationPercentage: 80
```

In this example, if the average CPU utilization across the Pods exceeds 80%, Kubernetes will scale the number of Pods between 2 and 10.

This section outlines how Kubernetes handles resource management, focusing on how resource limits, affinity rules, and autoscaling mechanisms help maintain efficient and scalable clusters.

5. Monitoring and Logging in Kubernetes

Monitoring and logging are essential to ensuring the health, performance, and security of Kubernetes clusters. These tools allow you to collect and analyze operational data to prevent, diagnose, and resolve issues.

Monitoring Tools

Prometheus

Prometheus is one of the most popular and widely-used monitoring tools in the Kubernetes ecosystem. It is an open-source monitoring and alerting system designed to collect and store time-series metrics. Prometheus is known for its scalability, flexibility, and power.

Prometheus Architecture

1. **Prometheus Server**: Collects and stores

metrics.

2. **Exporter**: Components that expose metrics from services and applications.

3. **Alertmanager**: Manages alerts and sends notifications when metrics exceed configured thresholds.

4. **PromQL**: A query language used to access and manipulate metric data.

Configuring Prometheus on Kubernetes

To implement Prometheus in a Kubernetes cluster, you can use the official Helm chart or a YAML configuration file. Here is a basic configuration example using Helm:

```bash
# Add the Helm repository for Prometheus
helm repo add prometheus-community https://prometheus-community.github.io/helm-charts

# Install Prometheus
```

helm install prometheus prometheus-community/prometheus
```

This command will install Prometheus with default configurations. You can customize the configuration by modifying the `values.yaml` file.

##### Prometheus Configuration Example

A `prometheus.yml` configuration file might look like this:

```yaml
global:
  scrape_interval: 15s
scrape_configs:
  - job_name: 'kubernetes-nodes'
    static_configs:
      - targets: ['node-exporter:9100']
  - job_name: 'kubernetes-pods'

```
    kubernetes_sd_configs:
      - role: pod
```

In this example, Prometheus collects metrics from Kubernetes nodes and Pods.

Grafana

Grafana is an open-source analytics and monitoring platform that integrates seamlessly with Prometheus to visualize metrics. It allows you to create custom dashboards for visualizing collected data.

Grafana Architecture

1. **Dashboard**: The interface for visualizing metrics.

2. **Datasource**: Connections to data sources like Prometheus.

3. **Plugin**: Extensions that add features and integrations.

Configuring Grafana on Kubernetes

Similar to Prometheus, Grafana can be installed using Helm:

```bash
# Install Grafana
helm install grafana grafana/grafana
```

After installation, you can access Grafana's web interface and configure Prometheus as a datasource:

1. Go to **Configuration** > **Data Sources**.
2. Add a new datasource and select Prometheus.
3. Configure Prometheus' URL and save the settings.

Grafana Dashboard Example

A Grafana dashboard can be configured to display metrics like CPU and memory usage:

```json
{
  "title": "Cluster Metrics",
  "panels": [
    {
      "type": "graph",
      "title": "CPU Usage",
      "targets": [
        {
          "expr": "avg(rate(container_cpu_usage_seconds_total[5m])) by (pod)",
          "interval": "15s"
        }
      ]
    },
    {
```

```
    "type": "graph",
    "title": "Memory Usage",
    "targets": [
      {
       "expr": "avg(container_memory_usage_bytes) by (pod)",
       "interval": "15s"
      }
    ]
   }
  ]
 }
```

In this example, two panels display CPU and memory usage for Kubernetes Pods.

Log Aggregation

Log aggregation is another crucial aspect of managing a Kubernetes cluster. It allows you to collect, store, and analyze logs generated by containers and services.

Fluentd

Fluentd is an open-source log aggregator that collects and forwards logs from various sources to destinations like Elasticsearch or databases. It is highly configurable and supports a wide range of plugins for log collection and processing.

Fluentd Architecture

1. **Input Plugins**: Collect logs from sources.
2. **Filter Plugins**: Transform and enrich log data.
3. **Output Plugins**: Forward logs to destinations like Elasticsearch or files.

Configuring Fluentd on Kubernetes

You can deploy Fluentd as a DaemonSet to collect logs from all cluster nodes. Here's an example configuration for Fluentd:

```yaml
apiVersion: apps/v1
kind: DaemonSet
metadata:
  name: fluentd
  namespace: kube-system
spec:
  selector:
    matchLabels:
      app: fluentd
  template:
    metadata:
      labels:
        app: fluentd
    spec:
      containers:
      - name: fluentd
```

```
      image: fluent/fluentd:v1.12-debian
      volumeMounts:
      - name: varlog
        mountPath: /var/log
      - name: varlibdockercontainers
        mountPath: /var/lib/docker/containers
        readOnly: true
    volumes:
    - name: varlog
      hostPath:
        path: /var/log
    - name: varlibdockercontainers
      hostPath:
        path: /var/lib/docker/containers
```

Fluentd Configuration Example

A `fluent.conf` configuration file for Fluentd might look like this:

```xml
<source>
  @type tail
  path /var/log/containers/*.log
  pos_file /var/log/fluentd-pos.log
  tag kubernetes.*
  format json
</source>

<match kubernetes.**>
  @type elasticsearch
  host elasticsearch.default.svc.cluster.local
  port 9200
  logstash_format true
</match>
```

In this example, Fluentd collects logs from container files and forwards them to Elasticsearch.

ELK Stack

The **ELK Stack** (Elasticsearch, Logstash, and Kibana) is a popular suite for log aggregation, analysis, and visualization.

ELK Stack Architecture

1. **Elasticsearch**: A search and analytics engine to store and index logs.
2. **Logstash**: A log processor and parser.
3. **Kibana**: A visualization interface for logs.

Configuring the ELK Stack on Kubernetes

You can use Helm to install the ELK Stack. Here's an example of how to install Elasticsearch and Kibana with Helm:

```bash
# Add the Helm repository for Elasticsearch
```

```
helm repo add elastic https://helm.elastic.co

# Install Elasticsearch
helm install elasticsearch elastic/elasticsearch

# Install Kibana
helm install kibana elastic/kibana
```

Logstash Configuration Example

A `logstash.conf` configuration file might look like this:

```plaintext
input {
  file {
    path => "/var/log/containers/*.log"
    codec => json
    type => "kubernetes"
  }
```

```
}


output {
  elasticsearch {
    hosts => ["http://elasticsearch:9200"]
    index => "kubernetes-logs-%{+YYYY.MM.dd}"
  }
}
```

In this example, Logstash reads logs from JSON files and sends them to Elasticsearch.

Tracing and Metrics

Request tracing and metric collection are crucial for understanding application behavior and troubleshooting issues. Tools like **Jaeger** and **Zipkin** are used for distributed tracing.

Jaeger

Jaeger is an open-source distributed tracing tool designed to collect and visualize request traces across services.

Jaeger Architecture

1. **Agent**: Collects trace data from services and sends it to the Collector.
2. **Collector**: Receives and processes trace data.
3. **Query Service**: Interface for searching and visualizing trace data.

Configuring Jaeger on Kubernetes

To implement Jaeger, you can use the official Helm chart:

```bash
# Add the Helm repository for Jaeger
```

```
helm repo add jaegertracing https://jaegertracing.github.io/helm-charts

# Install Jaeger
helm install jaeger jaegertracing/jaeger
```

Jaeger Tracing Example

You can configure your services to send traces to Jaeger using the Jaeger client for your preferred programming language. For example, in Python:

```python
from jaeger_client import Config

def init_tracer(service_name='my-service'):
    config = Config(
        config={  # usually read from a configuration file
            'sampler': {
```

```
            'type': 'const',
            'param': 1,
        },
        'reporter': {
            'log_spans': True,
        },
    },
    service_name=service_name,
)
return config.initialize_tracer()
```

Updates and Maintenance

Regular maintenance and updates of the Kubernetes cluster are essential for optimal performance and security.

Cluster Update

Updating Kubernetes is a process that varies based on the platform and installation method.

The general steps include:

1. **Check Compatibility**: Ensure new versions are compatible with your applications and plugins.
2. **Update the Control Plane**: If using tools like `kubeadm`, you can update the control plane with commands like `kubeadm upgrade`.
3. **Update the Nodes**: After updating the control plane, update the cluster nodes. This may involve restarting nodes or applying package updates.

Example of Updating with Kubeadm

```bash
# Update kubeadm
apt-get update && apt-get upgrade -y kubeadm

# Perform control plane upgrade
kubeadm upgrade apply v1.25.0
```

```
# Update kubectl and kubelet on the nodes
apt-get update && apt-get upgrade -y kubelet kubectl
```

Backup and Restore

Regular cluster data backup is essential for protection against data loss. Common methods include:

1. **Pod Data Backup**: Use tools like Velero to back up and restore Pod data and configuration.
2. **Persistent Volumes**: Ensure that Persistent Volumes are backed up using external storage providers or snapshot mechanisms.

Effective monitoring and logging are critical

to managing a healthy Kubernetes cluster. Tools like Prometheus, Grafana, Fluentd, and the ELK Stack provide deep insights into cluster performance, while Jaeger offers valuable tracing capabilities.

6.Kubernetes Use Cases

Kubernetes can be used to manage microservices, serverless applications, batch jobs, and multi-cloud and hybrid cloud environments.

Microservices

Microservices are a software architecture that breaks down an application into a set of autonomous, independent services. Each service is responsible for a specific functionality and communicates with others via APIs.

Advantages of Kubernetes for Microservices

1. **Automatic Scalability**: Kubernetes allows microservices to scale automatically based on workload. It uses the Horizontal Pod

Autoscaler (HPA) to add or remove instances of a microservice.

2. **Service Management**: With Kubernetes Services, you can expose microservices and manage load balancing between Pods.

3. **Updates and Rollbacks**: Using Kubernetes Deployments, you can update microservices without downtime and roll back in case of issues.

Example Configuration for a Microservices Application

Imagine an e-commerce application divided into several microservices: `catalog`, `order`, and `user`. Here's how you might configure these microservices in Kubernetes.

1. **Deployment for the Catalog Service**

```yaml
apiVersion: apps/v1
kind: Deployment
metadata:
  name: catalog-deployment
spec:
  replicas: 3
  selector:
    matchLabels:
      app: catalog
  template:
    metadata:
      labels:
        app: catalog
    spec:
      containers:
      - name: catalog
```

       image: myregistry/catalog:latest
       ports:
       - containerPort: 8080
```

2. **Service for the Catalog Service**

```yaml
apiVersion: v1
kind: Service
metadata:
  name: catalog-service
spec:
  selector:
    app: catalog
  ports:
    - protocol: TCP
      port: 80

        targetPort: 8080

    type: ClusterIP

```

In this example, the Deployment manages the number of replicas for the `catalog` service, while the Service exposes the service within the Kubernetes cluster.

Serverless Applications

Serverless applications allow developers to focus only on code, delegating the underlying resource management to a cloud provider. Kubernetes supports a serverless model through tools like Knative and Kubeless.

Advantages of Kubernetes for Serverless Applications
```

1. **Automatic Scalability**: Serverless applications automatically scale based on the number of requests, without manual resource management.

2. **Integration with Other Services**: Kubernetes can integrate serverless applications with other services and components in the cluster, such as databases and message queues.

Example Configuration with Knative

Knative is a platform that extends Kubernetes to support serverless application development and execution.

1. **Deploying a Serverless Service with Knative**

```yaml
```

```yaml
apiVersion: serving.knative.dev/v1
kind: Service
metadata:
  name: hello-world
spec:
  template:
    spec:
      containers:
      - image: gcr.io/knative-samples/helloworld-go
```

In this example, the `hello-world` service uses a serverless application image. Knative automatically manages scaling and load balancing.

Batch Jobs

Batch jobs are processes that run background tasks and terminate once processing is complete. Kubernetes handles batch jobs using `Job` and `CronJob` objects.

Advantages of Kubernetes for Batch Jobs

1. **Job Management**: Kubernetes manages the execution and completion of batch jobs, ensuring they run as intended.

2. **Job Scheduling**: With `CronJob`, you can schedule batch jobs to run at regular intervals, similar to traditional cron jobs.

Example Configuration of a Batch Job

1. **Job**

```yaml
```

```yaml
apiVersion: batch/v1
kind: Job
metadata:
  name: batch-job
spec:
  template:
    spec:
      containers:
      - name: batch
        image: myregistry/batch:latest
        command: ["python", "script.py"]
      restartPolicy: OnFailure
```

2. **CronJob**

```yaml
apiVersion: batch/v1
```

```yaml
kind: CronJob
metadata:
  name: daily-batch-job
spec:
  schedule: "0 0 * * *"  # Runs the job daily at midnight
  jobTemplate:
    spec:
      template:
        spec:
          containers:
          - name: batch
            image: myregistry/batch:latest
            command: ["python", "script.py"]
          restartPolicy: OnFailure
```

In these examples, the `Job` runs a batch operation, while the `CronJob` schedules it to run at regular intervals.

Multi-Cloud and Hybrid Cloud

Multi-cloud and **hybrid cloud** refer to using multiple cloud providers and a combination of on-premise and cloud resources. Kubernetes is well-suited to manage multi-cloud and hybrid cloud environments due to its portable and scalable nature.

Advantages of Kubernetes for Multi-Cloud and Hybrid Cloud Environments

1. **Portability**: Kubernetes is compatible with various cloud providers, making it easy to deploy applications across multiple cloud environments.

2. **Centralized Management**: It provides a single interface to manage and orchestrate

applications across different cloud environments and on-premise infrastructure.

Example Configuration for a Multi-Cloud Environment

1. **Cluster Federation**

Kubernetes Federation allows you to manage multiple Kubernetes clusters as a single entity. Here's an example configuration for federating two clusters:

```yaml
apiVersion: federation.k8s.io/v1beta1

kind: Cluster

metadata:

  name: cluster-a

spec:

  apiServerEndpoint: "https://cluster-
```

```
  a.example.com"
    secretRef:
      name: cluster-a-secret
---
apiVersion: federation.k8s.io/v1beta1
kind: Cluster
metadata:
  name: cluster-b
spec:
  apiServerEndpoint: "https://cluster-b.example.com"
  secretRef:
    name: cluster-b-secret
```

In this example, two Kubernetes clusters (`cluster-a` and `cluster-b`) are configured for federation, enabling centralized management.

7. Kubernetes Glossary

Kubernetes is a powerful and extensible platform for managing containerized workloads and services, which facilitates both declarative configuration and automation. Understanding its key concepts is crucial to effectively using the platform. This glossary provides definitions and explanations for core Kubernetes terms, along with examples for practical use.

API Server

The **API Server** is the component in Kubernetes that exposes the Kubernetes API. It acts as the frontend for the Kubernetes control plane, providing a unified interface to interact with the cluster. All communication within the Kubernetes architecture flows through the API server.

Example:

The API server handles requests from the `kubectl` CLI. For example, when you create a pod using the command:

```bash
kubectl run nginx --image=nginx
```

This request goes to the API server, which processes it and creates the requested pod within the cluster.

Cluster

A **Kubernetes Cluster** is a set of machines, virtual or physical, that Kubernetes uses to run containerized applications. It consists of a control plane and a collection of worker nodes (where the applications run). Kubernetes clusters are designed to be resilient and highly available, ensuring that applications remain operational even if part of the cluster fails.

Example:

In a cluster with three nodes (Node A, Node B, and Node C), Kubernetes ensures that if Node B crashes, the pods running on Node B are rescheduled onto Node A or Node C, maintaining high availability.

Node

A **Node** is a worker machine in Kubernetes, which can be either a virtual machine (VM) or a physical machine. Each node contains the services necessary to run pods and is managed by the control plane. Nodes run workloads, and their health is regularly checked by the Kubernetes control plane.

Example:

A typical node in a Kubernetes cluster might have Docker installed as the container runtime, a `kubelet` (which manages pods), and a `kube-proxy` (which manages networking for the pods running on the node).

Pod

A **Pod** is the smallest deployable unit in Kubernetes. It represents a single instance of a running process in your cluster. A pod can contain one or more containers that share the same network namespace and storage. Pods are ephemeral by nature, and Kubernetes automatically handles restarting them if needed.

Example:

A pod running a simple web server might be defined like this:

```yaml
apiVersion: v1
kind: Pod
metadata:
  name: web-server
spec:
  containers:
  - name: nginx
    image: nginx
    ports:
    - containerPort: 80
```

In this example, the pod contains one container running an `nginx` web server.

Container

A **Container** is a lightweight, standalone executable package that includes everything needed to run a piece of software, including the code, runtime, libraries, and system tools. Kubernetes uses containers (usually Docker containers) to run applications inside pods.

Example:

A containerized application might look like this:

```yaml
```

```yaml
containers:
  - name: my-container
    image: nginx:latest
    ports:
    - containerPort: 80
```

Here, Kubernetes pulls the `nginx:latest` image from the Docker registry and runs it within a pod.

Namespace

A **Namespace** is a way to divide cluster resources between multiple users or teams. It is a virtual cluster within a Kubernetes cluster, helping organize resources and allowing for resource quotas or access controls.

Example:

To create a namespace, you can use the following command:

```bash
kubectl create namespace dev-environment
```

All resources created in this namespace can be managed and organized separately from other namespaces like `prod-environment`.

Deployment

A **Deployment** provides declarative updates to applications. You describe a desired state for your application in a YAML or JSON file, and the Kubernetes deployment controller changes the actual state to the desired state. Deployments ensure that the specified number of pod replicas are running at all times.

Example:

A deployment for an Nginx web server with three replicas would look like this:

```yaml
apiVersion: apps/v1
kind: Deployment
metadata:
  name: nginx-deployment
spec:
  replicas: 3
  selector:
    matchLabels:
      app: nginx
```

```
  template:
    metadata:
      labels:
        app: nginx
    spec:
      containers:
      - name: nginx
        image: nginx:1.14.2
        ports:
        - containerPort: 80
```

Service

A **Service** is an abstraction that defines a logical set of pods and a policy by which to access them. Kubernetes provides several types of services: ClusterIP (accessible only within the cluster), NodePort (accessible outside the cluster), and LoadBalancer (automatically provisioned external IP).

Example:

To expose an Nginx pod as a service:

```yaml
apiVersion: v1
kind: Service
metadata:
  name: nginx-service
spec:
  selector:
    app: nginx
  ports:
    - protocol: TCP
      port: 80
```

      targetPort: 80

  type: ClusterIP

```

---

## Ingress

An **Ingress** is an API object that manages external access to services, typically HTTP. It provides load balancing, SSL termination, and name-based virtual hosting. Ingress allows you to define routing rules for external traffic that hits your Kubernetes cluster.

### Example:

An example Ingress definition:

```yaml
apiVersion: networking.k8s.io/v1

```yaml
kind: Ingress
metadata:
  name: example-ingress
spec:
  rules:
  - host: example.com
    http:
      paths:
      - path: /
        pathType: Prefix
        backend:
          service:
            name: example-service
            port:
              number: 80
```

This example sets up routing rules to forward

traffic for `example.com` to the `example-service`.

Horizontal Pod Autoscaler (HPA)

The **Horizontal Pod Autoscaler** (HPA) automatically adjusts the number of pods in a deployment, replication controller, or stateful set based on observed CPU utilization or other select metrics. This enables applications to scale out and handle increased traffic or scale in to save resources.

Example:

To configure an HPA that scales a deployment based on CPU usage:

```bash
kubectl autoscale deployment nginx-
```

deployment --cpu-percent=50 --min=1 --max=10
```

This command scales the `nginx-deployment` between 1 and 10 replicas based on CPU usage.

---

## ConfigMap

A **ConfigMap** is used to store non-confidential data in key-value pairs. ConfigMaps allow you to decouple environment-specific configuration from container images, making your applications more portable.

### Example:

Creating a ConfigMap from a file:
```

```bash
kubectl create configmap app-config --from-file=config.properties
```

You can then use this ConfigMap in a pod:

```yaml
apiVersion: v1
kind: Pod
metadata:
  name: app-pod
spec:
  containers:
  - name: app-container
    image: my-app-image
    envFrom:
```

      - configMapRef:
          name: app-config
```

---

## Secret

A **Secret** is similar to a ConfigMap, but it is used to store sensitive information, such as passwords, OAuth tokens, or SSH keys. Secrets are encoded in base64 and can be mounted into pods or accessed as environment variables.

### Example:

Creating a secret:

```bash
kubectl create secret generic db-credentials

```
--from-literal=username=user --from-literal=password=pass
```

You can use this secret in a pod:

```yaml
apiVersion: v1
kind: Pod
metadata:
  name: secret-pod
spec:
  containers:
  - name: secret-container
    image: my-app-image
    env:
    - name: DB_USERNAME
      valueFrom:
```

```
      secretKeyRef:
        name: db-credentials
        key: username
    - name: DB_PASSWORD
      valueFrom:
        secretKeyRef:
          name: db-credentials
          key: password
```

PersistentVolume (PV)

A **PersistentVolume** (PV) is a piece of storage in the cluster that has been provisioned by an administrator or dynamically provisioned using Storage Classes. PVs provide storage resources like disk space, which can be mounted by pods.

Example:

Here's how you can define a PersistentVolume:

```yaml
apiVersion: v1
kind: PersistentVolume
metadata:
  name: pv-example
spec:
  capacity:
    storage: 5Gi
  accessModes:
    - ReadWriteOnce
  hostPath:
    path: "/mnt/data"
```

PersistentVolumeClaim (PVC)

A **PersistentVolumeClaim** (PVC) is a request for storage by a user. PVCs consume PV resources and define the desired size and access modes.

Example:

A PVC can be created like this:

```yaml
apiVersion: v1
kind: PersistentVolumeClaim
metadata:
  name: pvc-example
spec:
```

```
    accessModes:
      - ReadWriteOnce
    resources:
      requests:
        storage: 5Gi
```

DaemonSet

A **DaemonSet** ensures that all (or some) nodes run a copy of a pod. As nodes are added to the cluster, pods are added to them. DaemonSets are typically used for logging, monitoring, or other system-level tasks.

Example:

A DaemonSet that runs a log collector on every node:

```yaml
apiVersion: apps/v1
kind: DaemonSet
metadata:
  name: log-collector
spec:
  selector:
    matchLabels:
      name:

 log-collector
  template:
    metadata:
      labels:
        name: log-collector
    spec:
      containers:
```

      - name: log-collector
        image: log-collector:latest
```

---

## StatefulSet

A **StatefulSet** is used to manage stateful applications. Unlike deployments, which manage stateless pods, StatefulSets provide guarantees about the ordering and uniqueness of pods. This is useful for applications like databases that require stable, persistent storage.

### Example:

A StatefulSet managing a MySQL database:

```yaml

```yaml
apiVersion: apps/v1
kind: StatefulSet
metadata:
  name: mysql
spec:
  serviceName: "mysql"
  replicas: 3
  selector:
    matchLabels:
      app: mysql
  template:
    metadata:
      labels:
        app: mysql
    spec:
      containers:
      - name: mysql
        image: mysql:5.7
```

```
      volumeMounts:
        - name: mysql-persistent-storage
          mountPath: /var/lib/mysql
  volumeClaimTemplates:
  - metadata:
      name: mysql-persistent-storage
    spec:
      accessModes: ["ReadWriteOnce"]
      resources:
        requests:
          storage: 1Gi
```

Volume

A **Volume** is a directory, possibly stored

on a remote machine, which containers in a pod can access. Different types of volumes are available, such as `hostPath`, `emptyDir`, `nfs`, and `persistentVolume`.

Example:

An `emptyDir` volume:

```yaml
apiVersion: v1
kind: Pod
metadata:
  name: emptydir-pod
spec:
  containers:
  - name: busybox
    image: busybox
    volumeMounts:
    - name: scratch
```

```
    mountPath: /tmp
  command: [ "sh", "-c", "echo Hello > /tmp/hello.txt && sleep 3600" ]
 volumes:
 - name: scratch
   emptyDir: {}
```

ReplicaSet

A **ReplicaSet** is used to maintain a stable set of replica pods running at any given time. ReplicaSets ensure that the desired number of pod replicas are running at all times and can automatically replace failed pods.

Example:

A ReplicaSet to maintain 3 replicas of a pod:

```yaml
apiVersion: apps/v1
kind: ReplicaSet
metadata:
  name: nginx-replicaset
spec:
  replicas: 3
  selector:
    matchLabels:
      app: nginx
  template:
    metadata:
      labels:
        app: nginx
    spec:
      containers:
      - name: nginx
```

```
        image: nginx:latest
        ports:
        - containerPort: 80
```

CronJob

A **CronJob** creates Jobs on a time-based schedule. It runs scheduled tasks, similar to how cron works in Linux. CronJobs are useful for running tasks like backups or periodic reports.

Example:

A CronJob that runs every day at midnight:

```yaml
```

```yaml
apiVersion: batch/v1
kind: CronJob
metadata:
  name: daily-job
spec:
  schedule: "0 0 * * *"
  jobTemplate:
    spec:
      template:
        spec:
          containers:
          - name: daily-task
            image: busybox
            args:
            - /bin/sh
            - -c
            - date; echo Hello from the Kubernetes CronJob
```

```
      restartPolicy: OnFailure
```

Job

A **Job** is used to run batch processes in Kubernetes. Jobs ensure that a specified number of pods successfully terminate. Once the job completes successfully, all associated pods are terminated.

Example:

A Job that runs a one-time task:

```yaml
apiVersion: batch/v1
kind: Job
```

```
metadata:
  name: pi
spec:
  template:
    spec:
      containers:
      - name: pi
        image: perl
        command: ["perl", "-Mbignum=bpi", "-wle", "print bpi(2000)"]
        restartPolicy: Never
  backoffLimit: 4
```

---

kubelet

The **kubelet** is an agent that runs on each node in the cluster. It ensures that the containers described in `PodSpecs` are running and healthy.

---

kube-proxy

The **kube-proxy** is a network proxy that runs on each node in the Kubernetes cluster. It maintains network rules on nodes and helps pods communicate with each other across the network.

---

etcd

etcd is a consistent and highly available key-value store used as Kubernetes' backing store for all cluster data. It holds the configuration and state of the cluster, and every change made to the cluster (such as deploying a pod or updating a service) is recorded in etcd.

Index

1. Introduction pg.4

2. Kubernetes: Fundamental Concepts pg.22

3. Networking in Kubernetes pg.37

4. Resource Management in Kubernetes pg.52

5. Monitoring and Logging in Kubernetes pg.68

6. Kubernetes Use Cases pg.88

7. Kubernetes Glossary pg.101

www.ingramcontent.com/pod-product-compliance
Lightning Source LLC
Chambersburg PA
CBHW071057240526
45471CB00016B/1982